A CLICHÉ A DAY

By

RL Gemeinhardt

Concept and Contribution by HR Gemeinhardt

Those phrases good and bad that show a bond as a society representing shared experiences and perceptions that you can review on a daily basis.

Other Books By R.L. Gemeinhardt available from Amazon

- Earth Dwellers Guide To Recycling And Environmental Conservation For Kids And Teachers

- Earth Dwellers Guide To Recycling And Environmental Conservation For Companies

- Earth Dwellers Guide To Recycling And Environmental Conservation

- Demob This!!! A Jack Owens novel responding to the Oil Spill from hell!

- Texas Used Oil Management: A Practical Guide To Compliance

- Author Web Site RLGemeinhardt.com

Address requests for authorization to VRM Group, LLC
Attn: Ron Gemeinhardt 190 — B2 Gulf Freeway, #126 League City, TX 77573

ISBN: 9798664819090

Prologue

This book is in part in memory of one of the authors, Helen R. Gemeinhardt, my wife and light of my life for more than thirty years until she passed away from complications of surgery at the young age of 49. This vibrant Puerto Rican woman was extremely intelligent with a zest for life and people who was struck down by serious rheumatoid arthritis at an early age of 19 and it proceeded to wreak havoc on her body for thirty more years, having countless surgeries, some successful, some not, and eventually one of them taking her life because of repertory complications.

What is more important to understand about her strength and love of life is that through it all she became a teacher, author, singer, musical performer, assistant director, mother of a child with Cystic Fibrosis for 12 years, and adopted a daughter with challenging needs. Most important to me, as we met in high school during a musical we did together, I was lucky enough to have her as my lover, wife, and best friend for 29 years sharing her life struggles but amazingly also witness to her always being positive and uplifting to all those who knew her and admired her strength, intelligence, and love of life.

Helen started this book shortly before her death and was more than 60% complete when the final surgery took her life but felt, as I did, growing up that a common understanding and effective communication relied on understanding the words and phrases we use as a culture that supports shared experiences and understanding. To facilitate this belief she wanted to share those Cliché's she loved with those of all ages to present her perspective as a single member of this blended culture and help others in all of society to at least be exposed to many of those they would hear by young and old as we all attempt to communicate with each other in this shortened forms of communication we now use.

This book tries to present many of the Cliché's most of the older of us have been exposed to in our lives but also adds some more recent examples that have been added to our dialogue as a culture.

To support her belief as a teacher of all age groups that knowledge was best absorbed in an organized routine manner and hopefully increase retention and maybe even facilitate use in your own communication she felt a daily format presentation might just do that.

INTRODUCTION

Webster's dictionary defines CLICHÉ as a trite phrase or expression idea expressed by it. Also a hackneyed theme, characterization, or situation. The original meaning comes from French and share's its definition with the French word Stereotype, both being printer's terms identified as familiar or commonplace. However, it is critical to note that the modern day definition of both are distinctively different as a Cliché being typically encountered by all and considered a reference to something hackneyed as a phrase being overused lacking significance, unoriginal and trite. Stereotype considered unacceptable by most, and especially by both authors of this book, is most frequently now employed to refer to an often unfair and untrue belief that many people have about all people or things with a particular characteristic.

This book is the authors reflections on the Cliché phrases we have encountered through our lives with added impact on our personal lives in an attempt to share some of the common ones in a daily exposure over the year. We both believe strongly that they have value to language and understanding as we communicate with each other in all forms and ages, backgrounds and different countries of origins.

A hope also for this book is that it helps all people in this country and others understand a little more about each other's references on life as many if not most are based on life's experiences as individuals and a society or representative of a culture and have a great deal of truth stated in just a few words and can often draw us together as a shared meaning to facilitate and effective communication of any kind and to the contrary perspective of some represent a lazy or trite approach to our communication. The fact should also be recognized that Cliché's change as culture experiences and references to the truths many of them represent change and are modified by those in the society the culture represents, young and old, and we tried to also present several of them here.

The perspective of some perceived obligation to be fresh and new in your communication miss, in our view, the more important need to effectively communicate with a well applied Cliché.

Author Note: Unless identified Helen's comments are first.

January 1:

"Today is the first day of the rest of your life."

This cliché use to annoy me. However, with age, comes wisdom, I hope. Now it is a reminder that every day, brings with it a new chance. Not just a chance to change your life but new hope that we all can make that change that will impact our life positively and those around us. **Ron:** Helen lived by this cliché as it was much more meaningful to her than most with all the challenges she had in her life I saw this approach in action throughout her life and believed it myself.

January 2:

"An apple a day keeps the doctor away."

A reference to healthy eating? This one has been with us a long time, hasn't it? May be really old but always true that healthy living will positively impact your physical life that can also have an impactful effect on your whole life.

January 3:

"To err is human; to forgive is divine."

Yes, we are all human – and yes, we all make mistakes. That's the easy part. It's the concept involved in the forgiveness of others that we seem to have difficulty with. Many of us find ourselves incapable of forgiveness ---not only of others, but of ourselves as well, moving forward often requires an act of forgiveness. Perhaps the toughest concept for most as many of us, especially those of use with a few years of supposedly maturity that can hang on to feelings that impact our life is so many profound ways. **Ron:** She was much better at this than I have ever been as she took a lot of harassment as a Puerto Rican and handled it far better than I did as a white guy who never cared about race and grew up that way just judging people by what they did or said and never cared about what race or orientation as a jerk is a jerk period. She forgave them all, and at worst felt sorry for them as she knew it was their upbringing that caused their perspective and she always forgave them and prayed for them along never letting her experiences impact her perspective of all people.

January 4:

"Something is rotten in Denmark."

This must be really old… but I heard people say this when I was growing up. I think it's a useful phrase when you sense something is wrong, you don't know what it is, and you don't want anyone else to know either.

January 5:

"Man does not live by bread alone."

You're telling me. Such a complex statement for such a few words as is does identify that we need so much more as humans to survive in any perspective of a quality of life. **Ron:** Another perspective on this is the "Quality of Life" is what matters and we agreed strongly that with her illness and our daughter's cystic fibrosis our lives where about experiences we could have together as a family and personally to enjoy our lives and reach that inner joy we all pursue.

January 6:

"Let nature take its course."

Natural consequences instead of manipulation and control. Sometimes we are wise to sit back and just let things happen. The challenge is always to know the difference between deciding if nature needs some help in its course.

January 7:

"Curiosity killed the cat."

Don't be nosey! This message comes across loud and clear to those of us who dare ask an unanswerable question… unanswerable (at least) to the person it is asked of.

January 8:

"Little pitchers have big ears."

Is this some kind of baseball reference? Maybe not. Another one of those parental sayings used to let adults know that there are kids around – watch what you say.

January 9:

"Better late than never."

Ah, yes. One of my favorites. Still bantered about today. It can be used sarcastically – I know you're late, and don't let it happen again. Or in appreciation -- I know you're late, but I'm very glad you are here.

January 10:

"As pure as the driven snow."

What is "driven snow?" Snow taken for a ride in the car somewhere?? Being raised in Southern California, I have assumed that whatever it is, it is a reference to something very virgin-like in its make-up and constitution. **Ron:** Being a Chicago raised guy this one is actually pretty well used in my world and does have true meaning of unaltered as to a person or perspective of a concept.

January 11:

"Rules were made to be broken."

This is the perfect rationalization for bad behavior… it should be spoken only in adult company. The adolescent will take it to heart.

January 12:

"I wasn't born yesterday!"

If someone implies one's ignorance, then this statement simply implies one's experience, intelligence and life-knowledge.

January 13:

"Laughter is the best medicine."

I read this first as a section in 'Reader's Digest' many years ago… and it is indeed true. Take it from someone who has had chronic disease and multiple surgical experiences … it always feels good to laugh. **Ron:** Helen lived this perspective as she always sought out the humor in life's experiences and had a great laugh that was contagious.

January 14:

"Experience is the best teacher."

Having known many individuals with advanced educational degrees, and admired many of them as well, I do believe that a degree alone is just a piece of paper. Doing, feeling and being a real part of something allows us to learn in a unique and very special way. Experiences become an integral part of who we are and doesn't every experience leave us with something? **Ron:** So well put and I agree with it so strongly from my perspective as well especially from working in a technical area all my life, speaking from a perspective of one who has a couple degrees.

January 15:

"Those that can do; those that can't, teach."

This is one of the worse statements I have ever heard! While those that *can* may do, those that *teach* are gifted and not only *can*, but *do* by sharing their knowledge and talent with others. **Ron:** One of those clichés that was probably written by a disgruntled person as I, like Helen knew several "teachers" that have in fact worked in the area they teach in and because they loved it so much wanted to share their passion and knowledge of the subject. She was one of them as she worked as a Medical Office Assistant and taught the course for years.

January 16:

"Don't put off for tomorrow what you can do today."

Why? **Ron:** Yes procrastination in all our lives sometimes gets in the way of our success and sometimes deep regret when it comes to actions regarding relationships.

January 17:

"Beauty is in the eye of the beholder."

So it is. Something that seems wonderful to one person may seem horrible to another. And while I think the original meaning of this phrase was directed at one's physical beauty, it can be applied to most any situation where a personal assessment has been made.

January 18:

"Nobody's perfect."

Thank goodness. Use these words when you have made a mess of something. It may induce the other humans involved to forgive you.

January 19:

"Make every minute count."

A reference to our mortality, this is a good rule to live by -- although it's hard to actually make every 60 second increment memorable --- make every day count for something or someone. **Ron:** So true, and I really believe we tried with our daughter and her Cystic Fibrosis that took her life just prior to her 13th birthday. I also tried with Helen when her health started to fail, but many regrets exist for moments or events I wish we could have experienced even with her wheelchair she was confined too for the last couple of years.

January 20:

"Honesty is the best policy."

In an era of situational morality and questionable behaviors, this is still appropriate. For as we all know, eventually the truth about any given situation comes out. Our leaders and politicians could learn something from this one.

January 21:

"A rose by any other name is still a rose."

Something that is, just is. Often we distort simple perceptions.

January 22:

"Keep on the sunnyside."

A very nice philosophy ----- sometimes hard to manage, but always appreciated. **Ron:** She always tried to live this philosophy no matter how bad things got.

January 23:

"Blood is thicker than water."

Scientifically, this is true. Whoever came up with this one was trying to make someone else understand that the ties that bind family to family are (or should be) strong. **Ron:** Some difference here with Helen as to family blood and those that join the family later and are not in the blood lines as it has been my experience that it is more like water for whatever reasons and is a shame.

January 24:

"Only the good die young."

A reference to the untimely deaths of icons like JFK, Robert Kennedy, Martin Luther King—and of late, Princess Diana. Although, good people die of all ages, it is particularly sad when death occurs before life has really begun. **Ron:** This hits hard for I lost two good people in Jillian and Helen that prove the point and died way too young.

January 25:

"That's life!"

Boy, I hate it when someone spits this out at me… I think it is said when one cannot think of anything else to say about an unexplainable situation… please; think of something else!

January 26:

"Fight fire *with* fire."

I understand that firefighters actually use this technique to combat certain types of fires… as for me, I prefer to fight fire with *water.* **Ron:** Helen lived this philosophy as she was a true migrator in all aspects of conflict and an inspiration to all.

January 27:

"If you have a dance, you've got to pay the band."

Nothing is free in this life… and anytime you have a party, someone has to clean up.

January 28:

"Kids are people too."

Not if they're between the ages of 12 and 17…just kidding … kids are just miniature humans and deserve the patience and understanding we commonly extend to adults…unless of course they *are* between the ages of 12 and 17!

January 29:

"What you see is what you get."

No hidden agenda here; not going to pretend to be anything I'm not. It's always nice to know exactly where you stand with other people.

January 30:

"Smile – it could be worse."

No. It really couldn't. **Ron:** So true when you actually do lose your child and wife things can't get worse. But I do believe that people should recognize that short of death that does not happen it is true.

January 31:

"Good things come to those who wait."

Exactly how long would that be?

February 1:

"It was love at first sight."

Now, how can that be? It's an easy thing to say after you've been married for ten years… but I've never known anyone to meet, and end up at a Justice of the Peace because they instantly knew (absolutely) that they wanted to spend the rest of their lives with a new acquaintance. Of course this could be why the divorce rate in this country is so high. **Ron:** Well, here is where Helen and I differ, as it was truly "love at first sight" for me as I saw her from a distance at a rehearsal of our first musical together and my life changed forever as I knew she was the one, nothing in our lives ever changed that first sight.

February 2:

"Life is too short to dance with ugly men."

Remember that. It carries more meaning than you think.

February 3:

"Love conquers all."

I would really love to believe this one as love definitely helps get you closer to conquering most things. But there are so many things in our lives that need conquering. Love cannot conquer terminal illness but it can make things easier. Our capacity to love is often greater than even we are aware of.

February 4:

"Take a picture – it'll last longer."

Sarcastically spoken to glaring eyes; eyes that seem incapable of looking elsewhere. It's true though. If you want a moment to transcend time, photograph it.

February 5:

"The truth hurts."

Sometimes this is very true for that which is revealed. But to the revealing the truth, I say "the truth can set *you* free!"

February 6:

"A woman's entitled to change her mind."

That's good… but I wonder why men are not allowed the same privilege? Reverse chauvinism?

February 7:

"He's/she's carrying a torch…"

Every time I hear this one, I picture a cloaked figure walking down a secluded path carrying a large wooden, fire-lit torch. This poor soul is in love with someone who doesn't return the sentiment and while the other person has moved on, our torch-bearer is unable to let go. The torch carried represents a blind, inner hope that maybe someday it will happen, I guess you never know.

February 8:

"You can't have everything."

And why not?

February 9:

"Make love, not war."

A popular sentiment of the sixties as it represented the attempts of a generation to make the world a place of peace. We have a long way to go.

February 10:

"A man's home is his castle."

Not anymore… and certainly not my home! It is a shared abode… shared with an equal partner …no king is living here. Ron: Kind of takes the air out of my sail as a man but true we lived an equal existence in all we did, even if I attempted to assert that male override on issues occasionally I knew she let me have the moment not that I took it because of some perceived right.

February 11:

"It's quality – not quantity that counts."

Oh – I don't know. I think it depends on what we're talking about. Sometimes *both* quality *and* quantity count.

February 12:

"You can't blame a guy for trying."

I suppose you can't blame a *gal* for trying either.

February 13:

"Beauty is as beauty does."

I heard a quote recently that was attributed to a 90's super-model. To paraphrase, she thanked God for her beauty. If He hadn't given it to her, she said she would have become a teacher. Someone needs to tell her that external beauty makes a memorable, but superficial contribution to the world. It is the beautiful person who engages the brain and *does something* that makes beauty matter… Like Princess Diana.

February 14:

"Love means never having to say you're sorry."

Wrong, Love means you make mistakes and should not be afraid to say I'm sorry. (Although, <u>Love Story</u> was a good movie). If necessary, today is always a great day to say "I'm sorry". Say it *because* you love them.

February 15:

"You don't know what you've got until you loose it."

Unfortunately, this happens. Most seriously, when someone we love dies. Take stock while everyone is still with you. Appreciate them. Let them know that *you* know exactly how valuable each and every loved one is. Do it frequently as this is something you will not regret.

February 16:

"One man's trash is another man's gold."

 Have you ever been in a thrift shop? It's amazing what people get rid of. A discarded chair, worn baby clothes, old china --- That chair becomes a college girl's favorite piece of furniture; the baby clothes dress a youngster's doll; and that old china becomes the only real set of "fancy" dishes a family has ever had.

February 17:

"Almost isn't good enough."

I think it is. "Almost" shows at least a gallant effort, don't ya' think??

February 18:

"Life is a bowl of cherries."

Cherries are delicious, except of course for those pits!

February 19:

"If mom says no, ask grandma."

This certainly was true of my mother and my children. It's a right of passage…moms who become grandmas get to spoil their grandchildren. Of course my grandmother didn't subscribe to this philosophy at all. I think that's why my mom enjoyed and was good at it…I miss her.

February 20:

"Anything worth doing at all, is worth doing well."

This phrase is used commonly by the older and wiser to impress on the younger and not-so-wise that tasks should not simply be completed; tasks should be completed with style.

February 21:

"Don't give up the ship!"

Fight on, fight on --- try, try and try again – but just remember; sometimes a compromise is just that – a compromise. It can keep your ship afloat. **Ron:** Helen lived this perspective as she fought the fight and never gave up the ship until her last breath.

February 22:

"With age comes wisdom."

Not necessarily. Look at Jesse Helms…

February 23:

"I'm on a roll."

Hmmm…this is usually a good thing. However, I suppose it could also be a reference to a not-so-good thing…anyway, it means that things are definitely going in a specific direction; one that could be difficult to stop.

February 24:

"Justice will prevail."

Here, in the nineties, we're not so sure. The system is the system, and as such, one might argue that it works, however whether or not it serves the purpose of *justice* has become a debatable issue. With the advent of televised criminal trials (like O.J. Simpson), we are beginning to question what we have long considered the best judicial system in the world.

February 25:

"Ignorance is no excuse."

It should be…

February 26:

"Real men don't eat quiche."

What the heck does this mean? **Ron:** Well, some men believe it is feminine to do certain things. I don't share the perspective as I like quiche.

February 27:

"Let's cut to the chase."

One of my favorite ways of saying "get to the point," stop rambling and say what you came here to say and quit "beating around the bush," etc. etc. etc.

February 28:

"Keep the horse before the cart."

Makes sense. Some things just naturally have to precede others.

February 29:

"The proof is in the pudding."

What proof? Whose pudding? Wonder where this came from? It implies that an issue of truth is at question, and that the *pudding* will clarify things…okay …

March 1:

"Lightning never strikes in the same place twice."

Now that's a lie.

March 2:

"Miracles happen every day."

I believe this … one only needs to wake up in the morning to understand the truth behind this phrase. There was a musical that spoke of "one-hundred million miracles" happening everyday…we only need to look around to find them. **Ron:** Her perspective shows here despite all the awful things happened in our lives she still had hope.

March 3:

"Believe half of what you see and none of what you hear."

Absolutely! One only needs to read the accounts of eyewitnesses at the same scene to understand that perceptions vary amongst us all. And of course you know what happens to gossip.

March 4:

"You can't believe everything you read."

Many of us think that if it's in print, it must be true. Pishtosh!! Pick up a super-market tabloid. **Ron:** Even more true now with all the forms of what you can read on-line.

March 5:

"United we stand; divided we fall."

What a wonderful phrase…and true. If people only realized that the strength of one voice added to others has the power to change the world.

March 6:

"Living the life of Riley."

Who's Riley?

March 7:

"Do unto others as you would have them do unto you."

Timeless… passed down from generations. Referred to as the "golden rule." I pray that parents are still passing this one on.

March 8:

"You are what you eat."

How depressing…especially if you love to eat. Of course if we open this one up to interpretation I might say that the more varied and interesting your diet, the more varied and interesting you are… the duller and blander your diet… well, you get the idea.

March 9:

"What goes around, comes around."

Hallelujah! Sometimes this is the only phrase that keeps me going. Especially when it seems like injustices are prevailing everywhere. Hang in there and you'll see, more often that not, this phrase rings true.

March 10:

"I am somebody."

Thank-you Reverend Jackson… (I think that's who first coined this phrase.) We are all *somebody*. We are important in a million ways, from the least known among us. Do you realize how meaningful something as simple as a smile can be? We all have the power to make a difference. Remember that.

March 11:

"God bless this mess."

I first read this on a tole-painted wooden plaque years ago. I have since seen it over and over again, and love it. I'm not the greatest housekeeper…and this helps me accept the fact that it's okay. Many women feel that if they can't (or don't want to) keep a spotless house, they will be judged by this fact only. God will still bless our homes, and it's okay to be great at other things. I admire today's *superwoman* who is a competent professional **and** great housekeeper. I've stopped trying to emulate her. I'm much happier.

March 12:

"In the wrong place, at the wrong time."

I really hate when this happens.

March 13:

"It's like trying to find a needle in a haystack."

I suspect that if one *was* trying to find a needle in a haystack that it would be extremely difficult, at best. I wonder if the individual who coined this phrase actually had this experience. **Ron:** Classic phrase yes and always implies the complexity of a difficult task or investigation into something.

March 14:

"It is better to give than to receive."

Oh, I don't know. I think it's nice to do both! **Ron:** Implied that one is supposed to get more actual or derived value from an act but I would argue it depends on the type of giving as if it is a material item then I would agree, however when it comes to knowledge or guidance it seems it would more likely be the one who receives than the giver, I know in my case regarding several issues it is true.

March 15:

"Things can't get any worse. And then they did."

Wow - Truer words were never spoken. I try not to use the *things can't get worse* phrase; because if you really think about it, things can *always* be worse.

March 16:

"If you can't say something nice, don't say anything at all."

My mom said this a lot. It sorta flies in the face of today's "express your true feelings" philosophy. So, let's compromise. State your feelings nicely. **Ron:** She agreed with this approach but with the qualifier as she could tell you about why you were full of crap without actually using the worse. It is kind of like using the phrase "you are skill set challenged" which really means you don't know what you are doing regarding an issue without telling you that you are stupid or incompetent regarding an issue.

March 17:

"A star is born."

The first thought that comes across the mind of a new parent. **Ron:** Yes typically thought of as a theatrical expression regarding a premier performance but actually can also be used regarding any activity that reflects a level of excellence that would be recognized.

March 18:

"What were we thinking?"

The first thought that comes across the mind of the parent of a new adolescent. **Ron:** Reality check as to questioning ones decision to act or not act about almost anything in life.

March 19:

"Make the best of a bad situation."

Why? That's often my first thought when faced with a bad situation, but the better side of me realizes that any situation is directly effected by my attitude towards it.

March 20:

"Get a life!"

A popular contemporary phrase applicable to the most annoying of people.

March 21:

"We're not in Kansas anymore."

From the WIZARD OF OZ … most of us have grown up with this one. It came to my mind when we relocated our lives from California to Texas… need I say more? **Ron:** Yes we both agreed on this for many years and was not for several more years after her death going back to California and feeling the same in reverse about the place now, proving it is not really where you are from and what you are used to but where you are going that has the impact.

March 22:

"Break a leg."

Doing high school theatre, I heard this one bantered about constantly. I don't really understand where it originated or what its initial intent was… I always hated saying it…I certainly didn't want any of my fellow cast members to *break* anything. **Ron:** actually "Break a leg" is used in theatre to wish a performer "good luck" and reflects a theatrical superstition in which directly wishing a person "good luck" would be considered bad luck, therefore an alternative way of wishing luck was developed. Having done a lot of theatre in my day I have used it often and would not use "good luck". Okay, call me superstitious, not a problem.

March 23:

"Patience is a virtue."

How true! In today's hurried times, impatience seems to be a common denominator for most of us. We might have a few less ulcers, heart attacks and migraines (not to mention less violence) if we tried a little patience from time to time.

March 24:

"Where there's smoke, there's fire."

How many times have you said this one? I've said it a lot… Usually to indicate that what I ignore might end up destroying something. **Ron:** Also implied by the cliché is that signs of something happening, like smoke, usually means it is based on a fire source but also something minor going wrong may very well mean a larger harm is taking place.

March 25:

"Luck of the Irish."

Shamrocks; that pot-o-gold at the end of the rainbow… that's what usually comes to mind when I here this one. **Ron:** Well a little difference in what many may think because according to Edward T. O'Donnell "During the gold and silver rush years in the second half of the 19th century, a number of the most famous and successful miners were of **Irish** and **Irish** American birth. Same outcome as finding the gold at the end of the rainbow or gold mine.

March 26:

"Sticks and stones may break my bones but words will never hurt me."

They can only hurt you when you let them, unfortunately they can hurt. **Ron:** Helen's approach was normally to feel sorry for someone who was ugly to her and it always seem to happen because of some prejudice idiot because of her Latin look and even sometimes when they identified her as a Latin woman who was also intelligent, she tried to understand them understanding prejudice is a learned perspective and offered prayer for them to gain wisdom, my perspective was mostly quite the opposite and felt explanation of there error in judgment should be given a more direct rebuttal.

March 27:

"You can take it to the bank!"

Guess this means that "it's" a sure thing…whatever *it* is.

March 28:

"The bigger they are, the harder they fall."

Literally and figuratively true.

March 29:

"May the best man win."

It's the nineties… it should read *'May the best person win.'*

March 30:

"It's the cat's meow."

What the heck does this mean? Personally, I find the "meow" of cats annoying…however, when this is used it seems that it is referring to something in a positive way… go figure.

March 31:

"Free as a bird."

I love imagining what a bird in flight might feel like. It must be a totally free, unrestricted feeling to fly into an open sky… no barriers…no obstacles… close your eyes today and try it.

April 1:

"Ignorance is bliss."

April fools! **Ron:** She tried to be humorous but her and I always felt knowledge was better than ignorance no how much more emotional or drama might be created if one actually understands the issue or happening.

April 2:

"Try it – you'll like it."

Oh sure … usually this means that you probably *won't* like it…be cautious.

April 3:

"I got it straight from the horse's mouth!"

Interesting statement….when spoken it is suppose to convince you of the validity of a story or situation that you might not be inclined to believe. It implies the use of a direct source…as though this *horse's mouth* reference signifies unquestionable and reliable information. This reference always makes me suspicious.

April 4:

"You can't get blood out of a turnip."

Who would want to try? **Ron:** Okay from a practical sense you cannot get something from something else it does not contain and don't let your expectations think you can.

April 5:

"Take your coat off and stay awhile."

I heard this one all the time when I was growing up. You can definitely sense a tinge of sarcasm in its use. At best, those who used it thought it was cute…implying that your coat symbolized that perhaps you were waiting for an invitation to stay --- or maybe that you were *not* planning to stay long. Either way, I never liked hearing it myself.

April 6:

"You had to be there."

Often, the funniest of situations in our lives just simply cannot be described verbally. And try as we might, hysterical with laughter as we tell the story, the recipient may be as stone-faced as the Lincoln monument. Oh well --- guess you had to be there.

April 7:

"Easy as pie."

There is nothing easy about making a pie --- well, not as far as I'm concerned.   Of course, my husband thought this was a reference to pi – you know; the one in algebra… pi = 3.14… and I have never found *anything* easy about algebra…. So where did this one come from? Probably a reference to someone who only had to *eat* some pie – not make it or figure it out. **Ron:** Not really as I remember it but I could be wrong. Actually I do know of the origin which is that the cliché "as easy as pie" is originated from the word "pie," which was used in the meanings of doing something quickly during the nineteenth century.

April 8:

"The fastest way from one point to another is in a straight line."

How logical. Often, when we are procrastinating, debating, analyzing, scrutinizing, pondering, or wondering, the direction of that straight line may not be clear… it may be necessary to take a turn or two first.

April 9:

"Forgive and forget."

Every human being has done something he/she is not proud of. We all want forgiveness. If each of us has the capacity to forgive, then it is easier to be forgiven. I know how hard it is to forgive certain human errors but I do believe that the ability to forgive is one of God's greatest blessings, *and* greatest gifts. **Ron:** Yes she did to a fault at times but it was one if her great qualities as a human not to hold things against others.

April 10:

"Easier said than done."

(Reminds me of a musical we did in high school…isn't there a song in Pajama Game that uses this phrase?) Well, this goes without saying (no pun intended). Let's take some common examples: *All men are created equal….* or *Treat others the way you would like to be treated…*or *I promise.* Commonly said and commonly invalidated by actions. **Ron:** "I'll Never Be Jealous Again" is the song from Pajama Game the line is in and as she indicated it applies to a lot of things.

April 11:

"Stressed to the max!"

Man – this is *really* stressed. Living in the 90's most of us know exactly what this means…time for a hot bath, aroma therapy and a nice White Zinfandel….tomorrow is another day. **Ron:** Life can get to the point with all the things going on in our hectic life that add stress and it mounts up.

April 12:

"It's not black and white."

Nothing ever is.

April 13:

"He's a prince."

And what would that be exactly? The guy in Cinderella who walks around the kingdom carrying a glass slipper? Or maybe the prince whose kiss has the power to awaken Snow White. My favorite prince is the Beast in "Beauty and the Beast," for to me, he was the *true* prince.

April 14:

"Shop 'til you drop."

I can do that! **Ron:** Yes she could and thankfully she understood, other than Christmas and birthdays I was not along for the ride.

April 15:

"There are only two certainties in life; death and taxes."

Remember that today. **Ron:** Always looked at this with optimism as you can change your life no matter what direction it is going and not fall back on any excuses.

April 16:

"Quiet as a mouse."

Amazing how really quiet a small mouse can be scampering across the floor, undetected unless picked up by shadow or surprise, and then the utter turmoil that quiet little creature can cause.

April 17:

"Put a sock in it!"

Wouldn't you love to be able to say this more often?

April 18:

"She works like a dog."

Here's a misunderstood statement. I've had lots of dogs. Not one of them would ever win an award for hard-work. Fun loving as a dog; sleepy as a dog; lazy as a dog -- Those all make more sense to me… this must be a very, very old phrase when dogs were beasts of burden…I can't imagine. **Ron:** This can be a great statement in some references because one of the possible origins is a reference to farm **dogs who work from sun-up to sun down**, so optimistically it is that origin being referenced of these hard **working** canines. Unfortunately, it has another popular not so positive meaning referencing a **day labor or "grunt" workers** has also been referred to as **"dogs"** and is an extremely derogatory comment.

April 19:

"Keep your shirt on!"

I love this one – as though one's urgency might include the removal of one's shirt. Actually, I'd like to see that. It could be a symbol of *real* urgency over a matter…You need something copied immediately by the secretary for a meeting in 5 minutes: So, you take off your shirt as you approach her desk – she gets the message immediately and runs to the copy-machine with your stuff and is back in a flash – I like it.

April 20:

"Give me a break…"

I say this all the time. Kind of a pessimistic little statement, don't you think? It means that I'm really not an idiot so spare me the malarkey. When I say it, it is always understood. **Ron:** I loved to see how she talked about this statement she received often, as I always thought it came from people who somehow took this Latin woman for something less than an extremely intelligent, educated, enlightened woman. I don't remember being at the other end of this statement but a few times in my younger years because I think I understood the woman, as much as any man could understand a woman.

April 21:

"Save the best for last."

Some people like to do this with everything – food, outfits, sight-seeing. Personally, I can't see it. Life is too short – I like the *best* up-front, always. You never know what is ahead. **Ron:** So true, and we tried as much as possible to do the "best up-front" as we could.

April 22:

"Time is the best healer."

This is so true. The problem is that no one can ever identify clearly *how much time* will be required. So, as individually as we all take life's happenings, so goes the time factor. It is different for everyone --- don't let anyone tell you differently. Take *your time.* Things always look better, sooner or later, when we use our own clocks and gauges.

April 23:

"Into each life a little rain must fall."

And into some lives buckets fall --- from one who carries a very big umbrella.

April 24:

"You can't take it with you."

Okay – but it's not staying here! **Ron:** We were always committed to spending what we had to enjoy life now for a lot of reasons and even though we planned for retirement we felt if we cashed the last check on our death beds that was okay as long as the kids and we enjoyed life.

April 25:

"You can't pick your relatives."

Wished that we could …..

April 26:

"He was in the wrong place at the wrong time."

This happens a lot.   Sometimes we know it…and sometimes we don't. So many things that happen – airplane crashes, car accidents, tornadoes – they have no explanations –and yet in a simple attempt to try and make sense out of things, we attribute an occurrence to "bad luck" – simple as being in the wrong place…I think there's more to the plan than that.

April 27:

"Oh – It's all in your mind."

Well – of course it is. Saying this to me only makes my perspective or view stronger…I have a great mind.

April 28:

"Grace under fire."

More than the name of a very funny sit-com …. But based on a phrase that means poise and tact are being demonstrated under the most difficult of circumstances… I admire this.

April 29:

"Buy now – pay later."

Ah – what a wonderful concept! But very impractical.

April 30:

"It's a man's world."

Bull-pucky! **Ron:** To the point, on Helen's part as she really felt this was an idiot's phase probably started by a man and our ego based beliefs or woman who felt the damage of a society that allows this to be correct way too much.

May 1:

"Fresh as a daisy."

Daisies are pretty, and very fresh looking… don't you think?

May 2:

"Friends are forever."

I've been extremely blessed in this area… have had the same group of friends for almost forever. Wonderful people who are always there for me … my mother always said that if you have one real friend in your life, you're lucky. Well – I've had unbelievable luck.

May 3:

"Behind every cloud, there's a silver lining…."

Or another cloud just waiting to rain all over you….

May 4:

"Take a number."

Busy? People waiting for your undivided attention? Your boss, your spouse, your kids, the postman? I say, take a number -- I'll get to you when I get to you.

May 5:

"Change is good."

It's what keeps life interesting. So many of us get so settled in our comfort-zones that the idea of change is scary. But without change, everything stagnates…and one day you wake up wondering just what it is you are still doing here. Change something today – your route to work; your hairstyle; your standard luncheon entre, now, wasn't that fun?

May 6:

"Take the bull by the horns."

But be careful….most bulls don't like people grabbing onto their horns.

May 7:

"Don't burn your bridges behind you."

But if you do, remember: you can always go around.

May 8:

"It's a case of mind over matter."

Well – if you say so.

May 9:

"God works in mysterious ways."

Isn't that the truth! I have always believed that things happen for a reason, even though most of the time the reason eludes us. With so much crises in my own life – chronic pain, illnesses, and the deaths of loved ones --- I consider myself blessed. (Go figure.) I experience true love and true friendship on a daily basis – what more could one ask for? (To win the lottery??) **Ron:** Yes I agree with Helen but sometimes I wish the reason would be a little more understood. I have a strong faith and have to believe just because I don't know the reason it does not mean there is not one even though taking my child and wife must have a pretty good one that I hope to find out some day if I am allowed into heaven where I know both Jillian, Helen and other loved ones are.

May 10:

"Some things are better left unsaid."

Ok.

May 11:

"Step up to the plate."

And that's exactly what the Florida Marlins did in the 97' season winning their first World Series – a miracle considering that they were an expansion team of only 5 years. Just goes to show you how far you can go when you have the courage to *step up to the plate* and swing.

38

May 12:

"He/she needs an attitude adjustment."

We all do at some time or another. But recognizing *when* is the trick…

May 13:

"Hang it up!"

And I'm not talking about your clothes!!

May 14:

"It's what's on the inside that counts."

Really? Then why do we spend so much time and money on personal beauty products, plastic surgery and designer clothes? Could it be that what's on the outside usually gets evaluated by each of us first? And worse, sometimes what's on the outside keeps others from really getting to know the inside at all.

May 15:

"Underachiever, and proud of it."

Yuk! We owe this one to Bart Simpson…worn on T-shirts for a time across America. I wouldn't mind referring to this as *adult humor* – I don't like it when kids adopt this concept…

May 16:

"There is NO free lunch."

Even a free lunch isn't free – if you know what I mean…it has to come from somewhere.

May 17:

"I'm between a rock and a hard place."

So I'm pretty stuck, wouldn't you say?

May 18:

"The mail must go through."

This is obviously a very old saying, originating (my guess) in pony express days. The mail here in Texas is slow - very slow – but I suppose, through no fault of its own. It *does* eventually go through.

May 19:

"Let's put our cards on the table."

And show my hand? I don't think so.

May 20:

"Take the high road."

This puts you on top – in more ways than one.

May 21:

"Life will never be the same again."

We say this when a trauma occurs – but the truth is that once a day has finished, life really *isn't* exactly the same ever. The world is another day older; we have been changed by the smallest experiences – this is life's design.

May 22:

"It's anybody's race."

I love this – it makes me feel that I can make it there just as quickly and as proficiently as any other human being … of course I may need to take a different path – but I'm open to detours as long as I finish the race.

May 23:

"No more Mr. Nice Guy."

That means someone is about to attempt toughness … try a more direct tactic … or simply launch an attack.   When you hear this spoken, take cover.

May 24:

"I have a dream."

One of the most beautiful phrases of modern America – Thank you Dr. Martin Luther King.

May 25:

"Silence is golden."

Hmmm …**Ron:** So many people should heed this approach.

May 26:

"First things first."

Naturally…the problem is in deciding what it is that should go first. Often time's people don't share the same perspective on this one. Regardless though, order is important to the accomplishment of most tasks. Having everyone on the bottom step together upward, works best.

May 27:

"Don't rock the boat!"

Yeh…we might all fall in and drown… and then again, the risk of a little jostling might just send us in a better direction.

May 28:

"You gotta take the good with the bad."

Ah, the nature of living. Would that everything we experienced was good – There is an argument that as homosapiens we are not capable of truly appreciating the good without the bad …I wonder…

May 29:

"It's not where you start – it's where you finish."

SEESAW was the name of the musical where these lyrics are found – and so true!! Getting started is often the most difficult of tasks; but we have to *start* before we can even dream of finishing…"…it's not where you start, it's where you finish. It's not how you go but how you land." (Great words.)

May 30:

"America -- Love it or leave it."

Okay, but don't stop trying to make it better. I'm proud to be an American – but I also recognize that we have problems that need our attention. The advantage is that we have the freedom to voice opinions, popular or not – and opinions do not diminish one's love for this country. Where would we be if John Adams hadn't obnoxiously voiced and re-voiced his opinion?

May 31:

"What if we gave a war and nobody came?"

During the sixties, this was a popular sentiment. It does give you food for thought….so many Americans have given their lives in time of war …freedom definitely *isn't* free. When are we going to figure out a better way of resolving international conflict?   There *are* better ways….

June 1:

"That which doesn't kill us makes us stronger."

I first heard this in the movie STEEL MAGNOLIAS.   Experience has taught me that this is very true….I am strong – and I *am* a survivor.

June 2:

"The truth will set you free."

Always….

June 3:

"Life goes on."

Hopefully! **Ron:** Helen understated this one as she believed it strongly that life must go on no matter what.

June 4:

"Love is a song you sing in your heart."

This must be the lyric of a song or something….from the 40's? Maybe 50's? In the 90's love has been turned into pre-nuptial agreements and no-fault divorce – times don't always change for the better.

June 5:

"Father knows best."

I guess that there was a time when we really believed this…it was a good television show…but with so many single moms left alone to raise kids, I wonder what the child of the 90's would have to say about this one?

June 6:

"Money isn't everything."

Whoever first said this one *had* lots of money; I'm sure of it.

June 7:

"It's all for the best."

This is something people say knowing that there couldn't have been a worse outcome for some particular situation. When my 12 year-old daughter died, I heard this a lot… use care and thought before using this one. I try to apply it to less serious events….

June 8:

"God works in mysterious ways."

Yes – He does indeed…in ways we can never understand. But I suppose that this is what *faith* means – believing; whether we can explain things or not.

June 9:

"Have a nice day."

Yuk! Combined with the happy face, this saying was the curse of the 70's! – Or was it 80's? And I still hear it today! Sometimes, even *I* feel compelled to say it, and before I realize what I am saying, out of my mouth it comes! I think that this was some form of covert brainwashing designed to try and make us nicer people.

June 10:

"Everybody loves a clown."

I don't know about that – I remember the "class clown" getting into a lot of trouble….

June 11:

"It's a cruel world."

Sometimes, but mostly when we forget to stop and smell the roses.

June 12:

"The sun shines brighter on the other side."

Where would that be? On the other side of what? I think the sun usually shines fairly brightly in my own neck of the woods.

June 13:

"Pretty as a picture."

I never want to look like a *picture* …

June 14:

"Scotty – Beam me up!"

STAR TREK fans everywhere know what this means… and don't
we all wish at some time or another that this were really possible?

June 15:

"The eyes are the mirror of the soul."

Kahil Gibran – that's where I remember this from… we read a lot of
Kahil Gibran in the 60's. He made a lot of philosophical sense.

June 16:

"It's out of my hands."

Thank goodness! This is always a relief, isn't it?

June 17:

"I wash my hands of the whole thing!"

This is even better! When I *wash my hands* there is absolutely no
trace of my having had it in the first place.

June 18:

"It's nothing personal …."

Usually when someone says this it *is* indeed personal.

June 19:

"Don't burn your bridges."

Why not? Maybe I don't want anyone following me.

June 20:

"Truth is stranger than fiction."

Boy, isn't that the truth! I look at my own life and sometimes it reads like a badly written novel…almost unbelievable. But as I get older, I realize that everyone thinks this of their own lives at one time or another.

June 21:

"Think before you speak."

My mother use to say this to me all the time – and now with my own twelve year-old adolescent in the house, I find *myself* saying this too….it's a good rule for all of us to follow…although, often we don't and end up hurting someone's feelings -- or worse.

June 22:

"What a worry wart!"

Let's break this one down…. To *worry;* to fret or think about probable outcomes -- wart; a dark skin elevation – not very pretty, is it? Get the picture??

June 23:

"Dead as a doornail…"

I think that this refers to an atmosphere, attitude or feeling…I hope that it wasn't an original reference to a human being.

June 24:

"Light as a feather."

That's pretty light, wouldn't you say?

June 25:

"Just say no."

Nancy Reagan coined this phrase in her fight against drugs. Some people made fun of the simplicity of this statement….I admired it....and still do. It really *is* that simple. It's <u>after</u> the choice is made that the hard part starts.

June 26:

"Getting by on a wing and a prayer."

Yes, I do this a lot…but sometimes that's all I need.

June 27:

"It's the tail wagging the dog."

Control. That's what I think this refers to – my dog always maintains control of *her* tail.

June 28:

"Tough tacos!" Or "Tough tomatoes!"

Ever try to eat one of these??

June 29:

"You're not the center of the universe."

Maybe not, but I AM the center of MY universe.

June 30:

"The world does not revolve around you!"

MY world does! Doesn't yours?

July 1:

"In the eye of the storm."

Not a good place to be.

July 2:

"You can never be too rich or too thin."

Too *rich,* no…too *thin,* yes.

July 3:

"The walls have ears."

I use to hear this reference made about children by adults….but it is very appropriate in today's world of cubicles, side-by-side offices etc. Be careful –

July 4:   *"Let freedom ring."*

Patriotic and wonderful!

July 5:

"She/he carries the weight of the world on his/her shoulders."

We all know someone like this. We've probably all been here too. It's nice to help someone who is in the midst of trying to do this….

July 6:

"What goes up, must come down."

Metaphorically as well as physically.

July 7:

"A stitch in time saves nine."

Since I hate to sew, it took me awhile to figure this one out… but I think it means that if you stop and take care of a small mess now, you won't have an unraveled mess later. **Ron:** A little clarification but basically correct as typically used to express that it is better to act or deal with your problems immediately, because if you wait and deal with them later, things will often get worse and the problems will take longer to deal with immediately.

July 8:

"I'm waiting for the next shoe to drop…."

This is *not* a good feeling.

July 9:

"Uncle Sam wants YOU."

No, he doesn't. **Ron:** Well, he did and still does if you want to serve in the military and was used a lot during the war years for WWI and WWII.

July 10:

"Don't kid a kidder."
Yeh! I'm smarter than you think I am."

July 11:

"Let's do lunch."

Cute phrase, isn't it? Modern, contemporary, concise and usually meaningless.

July 12:

__"You can't see the forest for the trees."__

This is one way of telling someone that they are so wrapped up in detail that the *whole picture* seems to be escaping them.

July 13:

__"That's the way the ball bounces!"__

And what way is that? Usually anyway except where you meant for it to bounce.

July 14:

__"Only the strong survive."__

Boy – ain't this the truth! Those of us who can continually pick ourselves up, dust ourselves off and start again are generally the ones still around for life's next challenge.

July 15:

__"Sometimes just thinking you can just ain't enough."__

I think I first read this in a Shel Silverstein poem; a takeoff on the original "The Little Engine Who Could." Most of us grew up hearing the story of that little engine who kept on saying "I think I can, I think I can …" and of course he did. But it may be just as important to understand that along with the belief, there has to be much more. That little engine didn't just "think" he could do something --- he worked hard to accomplish it. What if he'd fallen back down the hill? Would that mean that he'd failed? I don't think so ---

July 16:

__"Dressed to kill."__

I hope not. **Ron:** Well really not intended for the purpose of killing someone but of wearing typically glamorous or stylish clothes intended to create a striking impression.

July 17:

"What goes around comes around."

One of my favorites… sometimes it takes awhile, but experience has shown me that this is more often true than not.

July 18:

"Good things come to those who wait."

It is sometimes difficult to wait for the things we want. Especially in a world where we demand immediate gratification at all times. But if you have ever waited or worked or prayed for something that meant more to you than life itself --- and you finally get it --- there isn't a more gratifying or glorious feeling.

July 19:

"Money is the root of all evil."

This was probably first uttered by some poor soul serving time for major embezzlement or hustling. I guarantee that if suddenly I found myself with a lot of money --- it would NOT take root in the form of anything evil….pay some bills, help the family, kids to college, Caribbean cruise, Porsche ….. Well ---

July 20:

"Might makes right."

Shouldn't this be *right makes might?*

July 21:

"A day that will live in infamy."

Coined after the bombing of Pearl Harbor (World War II) --- those of us approaching middle age have a few of these racked up by now. My first daughter died on this day in 1990…..

July 22:

"It is better to have loved and lost than never to have loved at all."

Truer words were never spoken.

July 23:

"Give it some elbow grease!"

Now what the heck does this mean? I mean, I know what it was meant to mean --- but why? I can't think of two things more disconnected than *elbows* and *grease!* **Ron: elbow grease** is an idiom that **means** hard physical labor. The term **elbow grease** was first **used** in 1672; a 1699 dictionary of slang called it "a derisive word for sweat."

July 24:

"Everything counts."

First heard this said by Jack Nicholson. My husband is a great believer in this phrase. How wonderful if we all believed that everything we say or do really does matter…..it does you know.

July 25:

"You never know until you try."

You can think and think and think about something until you are pooped….but unless you take action, you will never know what might have happened. Remember, even failure means something --- you tried.

July 26:

"Anyone can be a father. It takes someone special to be a Dad."

Need I say more?

July 27:

"You've gotta have faith."

Faith is so elusive. It's invisible, lacks scientific evidence to back it up, and tends to waiver within us from time to time. When we believe so strongly and have no real reason to do so ----- *that's* true faith….and sometimes, faith is the only thing that can get us through.

July 28:

"We've won the battle; but not the war."

This happens a lot! At least when you win a *battle*, you live to fight another day. And, who knows – the war *could* be yours.

July 29:

"Spare the rod, spoil the child."

This is very old. It was spoken during a time when spanking was an acceptable form of punishment for bad behavior by children. Apparently, its ramifications were successful when practiced appropriately. It raised generations of responsible, capable and value driven adults. Today such an act is viewed by many as "abuse" when carried to the extreme, it <u>is</u> abuse. Many might argue that there are times when a quick swat on the gluteus will leave a lasting and sobering impression….one that may not need repeating.

July 30:

"It all depends on which way the wind blows."

Know anyone like this? No firm convictions --- no firm commitments --- says one thing one day --- something totally different the next? Feel badly for this person --- they really do not even know what it is they really believe in themselves… except maybe self-preservation.

July 31:

"Think positive."

Buzz phrase for the 90's. The power of positive thinking and all that. (It works, you know.)

August 1:

"You never know until you try."

Or you never try until you know! Works both ways.

August 2:

"You're never fully dressed without a smile."
-ANNIE (musical)

This was uttered a lot to me when I was growing up. It is part of a great number in the musical production of ANNIE….a slogan for a toothpaste commercial.

August 3:

"May the punishment fit the crime."

Unfortunately, this doesn't always hold true. In a society where fraudulent preachers receive longer prison sentences than some rapists, it would seem that priorities need readjusting.

August 4:

"An eye for an eye, and a tooth for a tooth."

Very biblical. **Ron:** Maybe fair to some but do two wrings really make a right, is not there a better way?

August 5:

"Freedom isn't free."

No – it isn't. Many have given their lives in the name of freedom. Our American democracy came to us at a high price from the Revolutionary War on through history. We aren't a perfect democracy, but we are the best democracy in the world.

August 6:

"Soaring like an eagle."

I can only imagine how wonderful this actually is. Close your eyes …. Let the wind lift you …. aaaaah.

August 7:

"This is the day that God has made."

And what a beautiful day it is.

August 8:

"It's not where you start – it's where you finish."

A phrase I learned from a Broadway musical, SEESAW. Life presents many challenges. Sometimes we have to start at the very depths of existence to be elevated. We do endeavor when we see life's problems as challenges. These challenges are what build our characters and make us better people.

August 9:

"One small step for man; one giant leap for mankind."

The moon landing! Can you remember where you were (baby-boomers and older) on the magical day when a man actually set foot on the surface of the moon? Outstanding.

August 10:

"He'd give you the shirt off his back."

Generosity, is a virtue my father possesses and passed down to his children. My brothers are just like Dad…generous to a fault….Could there be such a fault?

August 11:

"Close the door! Were you born in a barn?"
I get the part about closing the door, but what is the "barn" connection? I'm sure that my being a city girl has something to do with this. Do barns have doors? **Ron:** Okay, some more clarification as the original meaning of the phrase is traced to an exclamation of one literally leaving the door open. In olden days, and even now farmers often left the **barn** doors open during the day for livestock on pasture.

August 12:

"It's all fair game."

How primitive --- but challenging.

August 13:

"Wise beyond their years."

Many children are. Listen to them sometime. You'll be surprised at what you will hear when you *really* listen.

August 14:

"The devil made me do it."

Not a good excuse.

August 15:

"Sick as a dog."

How do you know? **Ron:** It unfortunately relates to a perspective that sick dogs suffer greatly and worse than humans because typically they are not helped.

August 16:

"If you don't like it, lump it."
When I was in high school, kids said this a lot. Just what exactly does "lump it" mean? It's not good, is it?

August 17:

"That's something to crow about."

Have you every heard a crow? I'm guessing this actually refers to the loud, boastful sound these birds make….. They do sound ecstatic, don't they?

August 18:

"Here today --- gone tomorrow."

My grandmother use to celebrate her birthday on this day. No one was ever really sure if it *was* her birthday, or how old she *really* was. She was a tough old gal who managed to survive the depression with money maintaining her independence at all costs. – and it cost her a lot. Family, marriages, and friends --- I miss her. I was so hoping that she would *get it* before she died.

August 19:

"Grow old with me, the best is yet to be."

Today is my anniversary…. Married over 25 years now and looking forward to retirement, travel and time. I have been connected to the best!

August 20:

"And on the 7th day, He rested."

In His honor, we do the same.

August 21:

"Mama said there'd be days like this."

She didn't say that there would be so many of them.

August 22:

"Works for me!"

A very 90's phrase ---- one of my favorites.

August 23:

"Give it to me straight."

Sometimes we *think* we want information without any frills.
Remember – sometimes it's the frills that make the information
attainable.

August 24:

"Nice guys finish last."

A mean guy must have first said this.

August 25:

"Dress for success."

A book by the same name was a big hit during my office days. It
contained rules to insure an appropriate and professional business
appearance. There is a belief that work standards of performance are
often linked to our standards of appearance. I think this is true.
There is a definite difference between attending a black-tie party,
and a luau.

August 26:

"The grass is always greener on the other side of the fence."

Ron: This is more of a complicated saying than one sometimes
assumes. The phase wants you to consider is that the grass is
always greener on the other side of the fence and expresses the idea
that **other** people's situations always seem better than one's own.
What should also be noted is that the proverb carries an implied
warning that, in reality, **the grass** is equally green on one's
own **side** and that you should be satisfied with what you have.

August 27:

"The ball is in your court."

Sports phrases are great, aren't they? We all seem to be able to relate to them.

August 28:

"My cup runneth over."

Is this another way of saying ENOUGH? Or is it a Shakespearean romantic thing?

August 29:

"Give him enough rope – he'll hang himself."

Most of us are capable of getting into trouble without the help of anyone else.

August 30:

"Face the music."

Approaching something, head-on. Usually dealing with an unpleasant or difficult situation, but often necessary.

August 31:

"It isn't the size of the dog in a fight; but the size of the fight in the dog."

So true.

September 1:

"Right makes might." Or is it, ***"Might makes right"***?

Well – there is a big difference. Think about it.

September 2:

"Straight as an arrow."

In this day and age, this could be interpreted many different ways…… I think originally it meant *straight* as in honest and forthcoming.

September 3:

"Laugh and the world laughs with you…cry and you cry alone."

This is not true. Not when you have good friends and family.

September 4:

"Only stupid people get bored."

Yep.

September 5:

"Three strikes and you're out!"

Sometimes this includes a few balls.

September 6:

"Feed a cold, starve a fever."

Or is it starve a cold and feed a fever? **Ron:** The quote is correct. It actually has some science too it even if not totally proved as accurate, but considering how long the statement has been used not too far off for its time.

September 7:

"He's got the right stuff."

Hope so. Ron: The "stuff" is what it takes to get the job done and a major reference to the astronauts.

September 8:

"I'm floating on a cloud."

Looking out the window of a 737, the top of the clouds look inviting, soft, plush and safe. **Ron:** Actually relates to more of a euphoria feeling of just being happy normally do to some life experience.

September 9:

"Suck it up, man."

Yep --- stop whining. Get on with it.

September 10:

"Sometimes good guys don't wear white."

It's sometimes hard to tell the good guys from the bad. They look and act a lot alike. When in doubt, trust your instincts…..that's what mama always said.

September 11:

"E=MC squared."

All things being relative, this is an undisputed fact.

September 12:

"Eat till your heart's content."

Some of us do this a lot....

September 13:

"What a low-down, dirty trick!"

That would be a *really* bad one.

September 14:

"You can't keep a good man (or woman) down."

Nope. They just keep coming back up.

September 15:

"Let the games begin."

This phrase comes from the Olympics. I use it a lot when challenged or when life presents one of those situations for which we must know the rules of the game.

September 16:

"It's anybody's guess."

Yes --- and it usually is.

September 17:

"Don't let the turkeys get you down."

You come across many turkeys in this life. The trick is to maintain your perspective.

September 18:

"I'm not fat ---- I'm fluffy."

I love this! What a nice and positive self-image. We are way too obsessed with body weight in this country. In many cultures, thin is *not* in.

September 19:

"There but for the grace of God go you or I"

We can apply this to many of life's awful events – when they happen to someone else.

September 20:

"Children are a gift from God."

Both my daughters are blessings …. There are so many of us who don't realize just how amazing this gift is.

September 21:

"Happy Birthday To You!!!"

Today would have been my oldest daughter's 24th birthday. Cystic fibrosis took her from me at the age of only 12… but how our lives were blessed by her mere existence. Hug your kids today. **Ron:** Cannot agree more!

September 22:

"Raising teenagers is like trying to nail Jell-O to a wall!"

Have you ever tried nailing jello to a wall?

September 23:

"School days, school days…dear old golden rule days."

We'd sing this song mockingly as the summer sadly turned into fall and we found ourselves walking back to school.

September 24:

"Friends are forever."

I still have friends from my second grade class! My mother always said that if you had one good friend in life, that you were blessed. I have had many --- and many long term ---- I am indeed blessed.

September 25:

"Actions speak louder than words."

Ron: This applies to individuals and especially politicians who seem to speak very loud and questionable follow through on actions despite promises made. It applies to all aspects of life.

September 26:

"Be true to thine self"

Ron: Can be a challenge for most and reflects that you should have confidence in your own perspective prior to judging others. Be yourself; be true to yourself; do not engage in self-deception.

September 27:

"The apple doesn't fall far from the tree."

Ron: Often said regarding children and their parents and how they act or view life, mostly good attributes but can most assuredly apply to negative things as well.

September 28:

"You can't judge a book by its cover."

Ron: As often true as we use our sight perception so mistakenly when judging people based on some assumed perception based on our own life experiences and you should always take a moment to evaluate you assumption as it can often be wrong.

September 29:

"You can't please everyone."

Ron: So true and we too often believe we must. Accepting that some won't be pleased no matter what your position or actions are is tuff to accept but as a phase above states what is important is that you are "be true to thine self" and then move on.

September 30:

"What doesn't kill you makes you stronger."

Ron: This one is supposed to give you optimism about bad things in your life that is supposed to present you knowledge and maybe even wisdom about handling issues in the future. Sometimes it really seems a waste of words on those that have a bad experience from their perspective, however from one of some age if you give it some time and really does happen. This one applies to you as an individual like the one above that applies to "us" as a group or family.

October 1:

"Love is blind."

Ron: Yes without a doubt at times and is many times at the detriment of the blind one who does not really see what is going on.

October 2:

"A mind is a terrible thing to waste."

Ron: So poignant and sad as we continue to not improve schools for everyone no matter where they live or don't provide the same higher education opportunities you have when you or your parents have money. We seem to be able to provide some opportunities to the top one percent no matter who you are as evaluated after high school but what about the ninety nine percent that may be able to develop if they would only be able to get more opportunity because it was not provided or life's issues got in the way.

October 3:

"There's no time like the present."

Ron: Always focus on what you can do now rather than put it off. Also to the alternative as we think of the great times in our past we must not lose sight on the present.

October 4:

"Better safe than sorry."

Ron: So true and I have spent a great deal of my working life trying to impress people on this issue as they do any work, because sorry is in various forms and can be minor but also life changing.

October 5:

"Rome wasn't built in a day."

Ron: Especially in these times many people should understand many activities take time to accomplish especially great things like the Rome reference.

October 6:

"A half-baked idea."

Ron: An idea that is either not complete or most off strange or even bad sounding to the other person.

October 7:

"A journey of a thousand miles begins with the first step."

Ron: So appropriate when addressing life objectives and informs one about no matter how difficult the task may be starting is what is important.

October 8:

"A leopard doesn't change its spots."

Ron: A cautionary statement regarding some people who are evil just stay evil no matter what chances or forgiveness they are given and should not be trusted. I happen to be a little more optimistic about most people actually do have the ability to change if they truly want to.

October 9:

"You have to kiss a lot of frogs before you find you're prince."

Ron: Tuff to convince my teenage daughter that a lot of frogs exist out there after that frog treats you bad, and you just need to keep trying because the prince will be there for you.

October 10:

"It's what's on the inside that counts."

Ron: Goes along with that it is not outward appearances that counts but truly what is how the person is on the inside that counts.

October 11:

"Good things come to those who wait."

Ron: Yep, but just how long do we have to wait.

October 12:

"Be yourself."

Ron: Pretty self-explanatory and a shame a lot of people don't head it. True quality relationships are based on you showing each other just that.

October 13:

"Do what you love and you'll never work a day in your life."

Ron: So true and as adults we should try to convince our children of just this approach no matter if we are doing it ourselves and quit worrying about material things as much. Often doing what you truly love and getting the skills needed will bring you all the money you need or at least enough to live and the personal satisfaction will be worth it.

October 14:

"Better late than never."

Ron: Being one that did accomplish things like my masters and writing my first novel late in life because life got in the way for a lot of reasons I was extremely glad I kept at it.

October 15:

"Reach for the moon… if you miss at least you'll land among the stars."

Ron: Where would we be if a great many people did not live this statement and the reality that having high expectations don't necessarily mean failure when you don't achieve everything you wanted to.

October 16:

"Let's touch base."

Ron: Yeah, right, if it actually happens.

October 17:

"Don't put all of your eggs in one basket."

Ron: Cautionary statement to always have a back-up plan as things may not go the way you want.

October 18:

"I'm like a kid in a candy store."
Ron: Loews is my candy store even at this age and I actually feel good when I am there, strange I know, but fact.

October 19:

"I lost track of time."

Ron: I do this often, especially while reading or working on one of my books.

October 20:

"A few fries short of a happy meal"

Ron: Well, should be an obvious comment if you have ever been aware of the limited contents in a happy meal for kids and direct meaning intended to express lack of intelligence on an issue or just plain quirky, unfortunately also used to express a feeling about someone not necessarily being too mentally stable.

October 21:

"We're not laughing at you, we're laughing with you."

Ron: Sometimes true but many times used to make you feel better when we all do something worth laughing at and a qualifying statement is needed hoping it is really meant.

October 22:

"Play your cards right."

Ron: Refers to any decision where multiple decisions are required to make something happen with a focus in most cases that all parties don't necessarily know what cards you are holding.

October 23:

"Read between the lines."

Ron: Oh please give me the wisdom to really do this as understanding the true meaning of some people's actions or comments often mean a great deal.

October 24:

"Beauty is only skin deep."

Ron: Another phases emphasizing you should not judge someone just by how they look.

October 25:

<h2 align="center">"Lasted an eternity"</h2>

Ron: To last for a very long time often referred to the love two people have for each other. When you put the word **eternity**, you can use it to describe a very long — too long — period of time, but also many use it to complain.

<h2 align="center">October 26:</h2>

<h2 align="center">"I am going to ship you off to Siberia"</h2>

Ron: Not something you want said to you as it means sent off to a far part of the world and part of Russia. Used by my mother when she was really upset with you or a warning for you to stop something, as a kid we knew we were in real trouble and actually did not know if she could do it but would not take a chance.

<h2 align="center">October 27:</h2>

<h2 align="center">"As brave as a lion"</h2>

Ron: Describes a very brave person.

<h2 align="center">October 28:</h2>

<h2 align="center">"As clever as a fox"</h2>

Ron: Describes a very clever person and is used to describe negative and positive actions.

<h2 align="center">October 29:</h2>

<h2 align="center">"As old as the hills"</h2>

Ron: Describes an old person or idea sometimes good and bad.

<h2 align="center">October 30:</h2>

"A diamond in the rough"

Ron: Describes someone with a brilliant future and you see people who fit this description in business and education a lot who show great potential with more training and experience.

October 31:

"Fit as a fiddle"

Ron: Not used much now but was many years ago to describe a person in a good physical shape.

November 1:

"As meek as a lamb"

Ron: When this is about you it indicates you are a person who is too weak and humble.

November 2:

"In the nick of time"

Ron: Something done just in time like many of my deadlines for lots of things. Saying is also relevant to any action especially when it comes to preventing harm or lifesaving actions.

November 3:

"Only time will tell"

Ron: How my mother often used this one when describing peoples actions and expected outcomes or ramifications of those actions and especially if we promised her something we would do consistently.

November 4:

"A matter of time"

Ron: Yes, sometimes you just need to wait to see the outcome, good or bad for it to happen sooner or later.

November 5:

"At the speed of light"

Ron: Definitely not literally at 186,000 miles per second most of the time but is used in reference to something done very quickly.

November 6:

"A chain is only as strong as its weakest link."

Ron: So true as it reflects on not only a team effort but related to any effort as a group. Primarily used to express that a group can **only** be as successful as **its** least successful or powerful person.

November 7:

"The universe will provide."

Ron: Akin to the phrase "God will provide" but more to the ethereal than faith based and part of the flower children culture where I first it heard. Realistically both may have value but you need to do your part as well, which is often missed.

November 8:

"Frightened to death"

Ron: My problem as a kid and still as an adult is horror movies that I have always felt they would do just this. Used a lot just to indicate being frightened a lot not necessarily to death.

November 9:

"Scared out of one's wits"

Ron: Okay, a version on the above that does not include death but still to the point of extreme fright and losing one's capabilities to cope.

November 10:

"As old as the hills"

Ron: Normally about old people but can reference ideas or concepts as well.

November 11:

"He / she was up in my grill"

Ron: In your face (grill) typically in conflict or even anger and not a place they should go, we all get upset over that kind of action. Also in current days it can mean someone being extremely vocal on a negative issue with someone not just a casual comment.

November 12:

"All is fair in love and war"

Ron: Not accurate from my view, both need rules.

November 13:

"Let it go"

Ron: Tougher than it sounds for many issues for a lot of people and usually used by others to address how you should handle something that bothers you even if you do believe it should just be let go it is often not just that simple.

November 14:

"The writing on the wall"

Ron: Presumption that something clear and already understood or is inevitable to occur because of the action or event.

November 15:

"Time heals all wounds"

Ron: Arguable especially when it comes to death of a loved one. Pain may lesson or you learn to deal with it but the presumption that pain and miseries will heal, with the passage of time is vastly over used.

November 16:

"Haste makes waste"

Ron: People make mistakes when rushing doing activities, opinions and especially doing political actions.

November 17:

"They all lived happily ever after"

Ron: Outcome following an event, not just a fairy tale.

November 18:

"Bag of bones"

Ron: Not normally a healthy statement about someone who appears very underweight.

November 19:

"Fall head over heals"

Ron: Usually in reference to love.

November 20:

"Waking up on the wrong side of the bed"

Ron: Based on the apparent fact that most people prefer a certain side of the bed where they do is that it's actually just easier for them to get out of bed on that side and when they don't they are bother. Pretty lousy excuse for being grumpy.

November 21:

"The quiet before the storm"

Ron: Based on the fact that weather events often have a period of calm prior to the impact of the storm and used often to express the lag time after an incident or expressed opinion gets known.

November 22:

"Between the devil and the deep blue sea"

Ron: Like being between a rock and a hard place where you mean that you are in a difficult situation where you have to choose between two equally unpleasant courses of action.

November 23:

"People in glass houses shouldn't throw stones."

Ron: So true for so many who come across as hypocrites when they state a dislike about someone or something someone does. Old reference based on the word of God about a challenge to those without sin cast the first stone, can't happen as we all have sin.

November 24:

"Chip on your shoulder"

Ron: Typically means that you think you're better than everyone else but also references a negative response beyond normal on an issue that is set off easily.

November 25:

"Do you think I am made of money"

Ron: Often used by parents with older kids but others as well when asked for something that the other can't really afford.

November 26:

"Old habits die hard."

Ron: Yes and I am guilty as many about doing things in a certain way and reluctant to change, no matter what the option because of stubbornness or maybe even failing to see the value. I prefer to believe it is because there are many ways to do things and I am just doing it in one way.

November 27:

"A picture is worth a thousand words."

Ron: So true especially in this day of cameras and phone video everywhere and how valuable the pictures are compared to what people report as what they say happened and how it more clearly expresses the event.

November 28:

"A watched pot never boils."

Ron: Seems true when you actually try it as our perception of time is impacted by internalized by expectations over the reality that the actual time is not impacted on more than boiling things.

November 29:

"Opposites attract."

Ron: I know this is true based on my attraction to Helen and is often referenced about relationships. I thank God it was so because she made me a better man and I could not imagine life with someone like me. I was fortunate to have the same great luck in finding my current wife Marilyn.

November 30:

"Any port in a storm"

Ron: Has a pretty obvious meaning in a bad situation, any help will do. Also referenced for a person who has many lovers and goes to one of several in conflict with one of the others for support, and often maybe not the best choice.

December 1:

"Don't cry over spilled milk."

Ron: Okay, so you need to suck it up and move on after something negative happens, not horrible because just the minor things in life and move on.

December 2:

"Gut-wrenching pain"

Ron: Describes horrible pain. I have had it only a few times in my life but have seen Helen with it and she dealt with it like a hero and it was my gut-wrenching as I watched her go through it. It can also reference an emotional feeling from watching someone else.

December 3:

"Love you more than life itself."

Ron: The phase many of us parents use about how we feel about our kids and would give our lives for them if that what was needed.

December 4:

"Weak as a kitten"

Ron: With a presumption that a kitten is weak used to identify a person or other animal's state of being or position on an issue.

December 5:

"All for one, and one for all"

Ron: Associated with the Three Musketeers novel and reflects a strong belief that each individual should act for the benefit of the group, and the group should act for the benefit of each individual. Good and bad use as blind allegiance to a group or issue has had some extremely historical harms. However, when done for good it can have an amazing impact.

December 6:

"With experience comes wisdom, and with wisdom comes experience"

Ron: It is really not true for everyone despite what logic should tell you. I have seen many people with a lot of experience in an area and either were not really paying attention or learn from their experiences and made the same mistakes or reflect any wisdom.

December 7:

"Acid test"

Ron: One of my favorites as it refers to a test which will either prove or disprove the truth or worth of something.

December 8:

"There are no words."

Ron: Accurate to some point, especially at the loss of a child but some words are always helpful. Also used when something is so bad no words make sense to explain how bad something is.

December 9:

"I'm efforting that as we speak."

Ron: Fancy way to say I am working on it right now.

December 10:

"We should workshop that idea."

Ron: Okay, company talk indicating we should have a long session on that issue to refine the idea or plan.

December 11:

"We should make sure we're on the same page."

Ron: Tactful way of saying I am not sure we are in agreement and we need to talk more.

December 12:

"At the end of the day..."

Ron: Normally something that you say before you give the most important fact of a situation and also presented prior to given the final statement of a result or position held.

December 13:

"It is what it is"

Ron: Given as a statement to identify your need to accept what you are told.

December 14:

"Epic fail". Or "epic" anything.

Ron: It is really big or bad and stands out in history.

December 15:

"Own it."
Ron: You need to take responsibility for your decisions and or actions.

December 16:

"That's so last century."

Ron: Okay, so you need to get updated on your view or statement about something.

December 17:

"Early to bed and early to rise makes a man

healthy, wealthy and wise."

Ron: One from Ben Franklin's farmer's almanac that my mother used a lot and still has value to express how important rest is and getting an early start usually enhances your chances of more success as you live a healthy life.

December 18:

"At least she didn't suffer." "At least she's not suffering anymore."

Ron: Used to help us feel better about a death. Believing strongly in the quality of life this one is one I have relied on a lot with the suffering deaths of both my wife and daughter adding some comfort.

December 19:

"Don't overthink it."

Ron: I am guilty of this a lot and presents a cautionary statement as most things are pretty obvious as to what is needed without dragging out the process to determine actions or resolution and often leads to a lousy result.

December 20:

"There are no gains without pains."

Ron: From Benjamin Franklin and can apply to a lot of things in life not just political or exercise but lots of roads to goals or object involve pain (not necessarily physical) to get were you or a country, community need to go.

December 21:

"You killed it last night"; "You really nailed it."

Ron: You really did a good job.

December 22:

"My career's really blowing up." Or "exploding."

Ron: Things are going well for you as to your job.

December 23:

"That doesn't resonate as much as it used to." "It's palpable."

Ron: Your meaning or result is not as impactful as it used to be.

December 24:

"I didn't sign up for that."

Ron: Something you want me to do that was not a presumed part of my agreement with you or the company as to what I am required to do.

December 25:

"That's a bottomless pit."

Ron: More problems or harm than is reasonable and has no clear end or yet to be understandable harm.

December 26:

"Don't get bent out of shape over it."

Ron: You should not be too excited or upset over something and accept it.

December 27:

"Baby daddy" or "baby mommy"

Ron: Identifies a baby-daddy or baby-mama as someone you have a child with, and to whom you were never married. Hopefully but often not involved in the child's life, but have no romantic relationship with the other parent.

December 28:

"I can't wrap my mind around that."

Ron: Admitting you can't understand why something was done and could be an idea or action.

December 29:

"It's the elephant in the room."

Ron: Something that is normally obvious to all involved but reluctant to deal with. The elephant normally represents a difficult situation or unpleasant experiences related to the issue.

December 30:

"Sorry, that's not really in my wheelhouse."

Ron: Something I don't know how to do or believe is not my responsibility.

December 31:

"Pity party"

Ron: Reference to an instance of feeling sorry for oneself or seeking **pity** from other people. Normally a negative connotation to how you are acting.